To Alf.

Lots of love always

Margaret

Summer 2014

THE *NEW*
UXBRIDGE
ENGLISH DICTIONARY

The NEW UXBRIDGE ENGLISH DICTIONARY is indebted to Rob Brydon, Jack Dee, Stephen Fry, Andy Hamilton, Jeremy Hardy, Tony Hawks, Ross Noble and Sandi Toksvig for their invaluable contributions to this book, and to Colin Hall and Tony McSweeney for their excellent illustrations.

HarperCollins*Publishers*
77–85 Fulham Palace Road,
Hammersmith, London W6 8JB
www.harpercollins.co.uk

First published by HarperCollins*Publishers* 2008

8

© Tim Brooke-Taylor, Barry Cryer, Graeme Garden,
Jon Naismith and Iain Pattinson

The authors assert the moral right to be
identified as the authors of this work

Illustrations by Tony McSweeney

A catalogue record of this book is
available from the British Library

ISBN-13 978-0-00-726393-6
ISBN-10 0-00-726393-7

Printed and bound in Great Britain by
Clays Ltd, St Ives plc

Picture Credit: p5 Tim Rooke/Rex Features

All rights reserved. No part of this publication may be
reproduced, stored in a retrieval system, or transmitted,
in any form or by any means, electronic, mechanical,
photocopying, recording or otherwise, without the prior
written permission of the publishers.

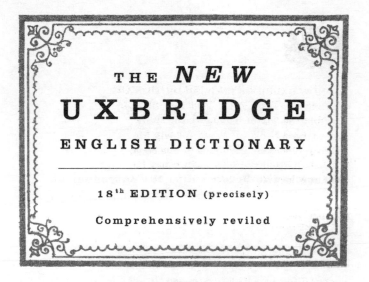

THE *NEW* UXBRIDGE

ENGLISH DICTIONARY

18ᵗʰ EDITION (precisely)

Comprehensively reviled

TIM BROOKE-TAYLOR
BARRY CRYER
GRAEME GARDEN
JON NAISMITH
IAIN PATTINSON

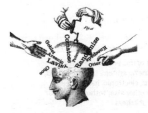

THE *NEW*
UXBRIDGE
ENGLISH DICTIONARY

A COMPANION TO THE ORIGINAL UXBRIDGE ENGLISH DICIONARY

CONTAINING OVER 600 NEW DEFINITIONS

Preface to the Foreword to the Introduction

It was the runaway commercial success of the Uxbridge English Dictionary that allowed the University of Uxbridge to build its new Library, and now, thanks to unexpected lottery funding (three scratch cards in one week – uncanny!) the Library Extension has been completed. A generous donation of books from TV's Jeremy Kyle has almost filled up the shelf.

Research carried on in the English Department of the University has resulted in the production of this volume updating and clarifying the definitions of many hitherto misunderstood words.

Foreword to the Introduction

English speakers are blessed with a remarkably rich language. Indeed every year the *Sunday Times* List of the '100 Richest Languages' is regularly topped by English, with Mandarin a plucky second. But what is it that gives our mother tongue this unsurpassed richness? Quite simply it is the words. Our language is chock full of them. In fact there are more words in the Complete English Dictionary than there are grains of sand.

Her Majesty the Queen digging up a tree to make way for the new Library Extension.

Introduction

The earliest alphabets come down to us from the Bronze Age, when there were few words but everyone sported a healthy suntan. The Phoenicians had an alphabet before they had any words at all, and each letter contained a wealth of meaning. Even today, when we send a message we speak of sending a 'letter'. Eventually these single letters became combined to form words, and from that point onwards the complexities of language ensured an almost infinite capacity for misunderstanding.

Early civilizations, which had managed perfectly well communicating by letters alone, were at first overwhelmed by the arrival of these bulky and hard-to-understand 'words'. It was a long time before they were adopted as part of language, being heavy and hard to manage for the inexperienced Greeks and even Romans, who would use them as fodder for their domestic animals, lagging for hypocausts or even doorstops. A proper use for words was not actually discovered until the 1920s when they were found to be ideal for filling in the crossword grids published in the better class of newspaper. In a matter of months words had found their way out of the crosswords and into the rest of the newspaper, and before long they were to be found in books and magazines and on parking tickets.

Like it or not, words are here to stay, and we in the department are dedicated to their proper usage. We hope this slim volume will help you to enrich your use of language and avoid linguistic pitfalls.

Warmest facilitations
from

THE EDITOR

N.V.Q. De Ploma
(Dean, Vice-Chancellor, Remedial Metalwork) University of Uxbridge

Aa

fig.1 Archive

Aa

Aberdare
to challenge Benny, Björn, Agnetha
and Anni-Frid

Acapulco
Mexican clarinet player

Acne
a walking stick for dyslexics

Aerobic
chocolate biro

Aerospace
room for more chocolate

Aggregate
farming scandal

Aberdare–Amstrad

Agog
a half-finished Jewish temple

A la carte
a Muslim wheelbarrow

Alimony
with lemon

Already
to suffer from
sunburn

Amish
rather like an arm

fig.2 A la carte

Amstrad
amateur violinist

Aa

Analogy
something that makes you itchy
and sneezy

Analyse
to examine someone's backside

Animate
to grow too fond of your pets

Annex
Captain Mark Phillips

Appetite
cheerfully drunk

Approximate
a mistress

fig.3 Analyse

Analogy–Arson

Arboretum
a dockside restaurant

Archive
where Noah kept his bees

Argy-bargy
owner of a narrow boat
in Buenos Aires

Arrest
that long stick thing
they use in snooker

Arsenic
to steal buttocks

Arson
to sit

fig. 4 Appetite

Aa

Artichoke
1. to suppress a cough while at the theatre; 2. to strangle Brian Sewell

Artifact
Tracy Emin is rubbish

Artistry
History of Art

Asbestos
Greek Anti Social Behaviour Order

ASBO
is courting

Asperger's syndrome
a tendency to overuse laxatives

fig.5 Asbestos

Assert

a sure winner

Asshole

suddenly remembering the capital of
South Korea

Asthmatic

electric bidet

Audi A4

what you say when you drop a
heavy ream of paper on your foot

Automat

October headwear

AWOL

dyslexic owl

fig.6 Audi A4

Bb

fig. 7 Bearings

THE NEW UXBRIDGE ENGLISH DICTIONARY

Bacchanalian
to bet on an outsider in the space race

Badinage
dyslexic bandage

Baghdad
Ann Widdecombe's father

fig.8 Barbecue

Baltic
involuntary testicular spasm

Baltimore
to ask for seconds in an Indian restaurant

Barbecue
long wait for a haircut

Barman
a superhero who never quite notices anybody

Bb

Battleaxe
a boon for constipated bats

Bauhaus
Buckingham Palace

Bearings
Yogi's jewellery

Beforehand
insect tennis stroke

fig.9 Beforehand

Beginnings
a century at Lords

Benign
what it'll be after eight

Bias
the street cry of American rent boys

Battleaxe–Bleach

Biceps
sexually ambivalent mushrooms

Bigamy
that shows magnanimity on my part

Binge
where Sean Connery puts his rubbish

Binmen
people that were male but are now female

Biosphere
to purchase a ball

Birkenhead
Merseyside body snatchers

fig. 10 Binmen

Bleach
a hole in the Great Wall of China

Bb

Bloater
Japanese straw hat

Blogger
computer-literate lumberjack

Bordeaux
to piss off a deer

Botox
a seafaring bullock

fig. 11 Botox

Briar patch
something to help you overcome
your craving for thickets

Broadband
no fatties please

Brocade
medical assistance for badgers

Bronchodilator
a very old horse

Brouhaha
a cup of tea that tastes funny

Buffalo
popular greeting at nudist camp

Buggery
the study of insects

Burnish
a bit like a burn

Buzzard
energetic panel game

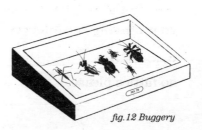

fig. 12 Buggery

Cc

fig.13 Celtic

Cabin–Cannibals

Cabin
the taxi's arrived

Cabriolet
milk chocolate

Cacti
rubbish neckwear

Caesarean section
part of a salad

fig.14 Cacti

Canapé
Scottish inability to settle one's bills

Cannelloni
Scot's refusal to give one an overdraft

Cannibals
strangely intelligent Scottish cattle

Cc

Cardiac
somebody who knows a hell of a lot about cardigans

Carmelite
half-hearted Buddhist

Carping
imitating a fish

Cashew
a nut that makes you sneeze

Castanets
what Italian fishermen do

Catastrophe
feline punctuation

Catharsis
bums on seats at Mass

fig.15 Carping

Celtic
a prison for fleas

Chaff
a posh chav

Château
cat's piss

fig.16 Chipmunk

Chauffeur
a mink salesman

Cheapskate
a fish that does budgie impressions

Chinchilla
an air-conditioned beard

Chipmunk
a friar

Cc

Chiropractice
getting ready to go to Egypt

Circumflex
to cut the end off a piece of wire

fig. 17 Chiropractice

Claimant
an insect that's had an accident at work

Clarity
a bit like red wine

Climate
first instruction at mountaineering school

Climax
scale the north face of Mr Bygraves

Cloak
cry of a Chinese frog

Chiropractice–Cloak

fig.18 Chinchilla

Cc

Cloister
a pretentious clam

Cocker spaniel
at your peril

Cockney
damage to the patella from a long penis

Coconut
chocoholic

Codicil
this fish is unwell

fig. 19 Codicil

Coitus interruptus
deck games on the *Titanic*

Collier
like a collie but even more so

Cloister–Concurrent

Colliery
sort of like a collie but even more so

Collywobbles
that dog's pissed

Comatose
what a beautician does to a lady with a lot of
unwanted hair

Commonplace
Essex

Conceited
a prisoner on a chair

Concurrent
an object that looks
like a raisin, but isn't

fig.20 Comatose

Cc

Cormorants
Good heavens! Extra insects

Corsage
Blimey, it's a copper

Counterpane
someone working in the Post Office

County Down
a Chinese space launch

Crackerjack
a device for raising biscuits

Crème brûlée
the crematorium's on fire

Crocus
a foul-mouthed blackbird

fig.21 Cormorants

Cormorants–Cyrillic

Cruise control
Scientology

fig.22 Crocus

Cuckold
so chilly you stutter

Curator
someone who assesses snooker equipment

Curlicue
Welsh dog

Cursory
where small children learn to swear

Cuticle
sexual harassment at the Post Office

Cyrillic
similar to Cyril

Dd

fig.23 Defamatory

Damnation–Decanter

Damnation
Holland

Dashboard
selectors for the 100 metres

Database
place where Lonely Hearts hang out

Daunting
an alarm clock

Dayglo
shiny Spaniard

Decade
Ant

Decanter
Italian for gallop

fig.24 Damnation

Dd

Decrease
do the ironing

Defamatory
hard of hearing but still frisky

fig. 25 Decrease

Defective
policeman with a speech impediment

Definite
street slang for 'hard of hearing'

Defunct
to have one's sense of rhythm removed

Defuse
as used in de plug

Delaware
to have seen *Only Fools and Horses*

Decrease–Diabetes

Delegate
Jewish scandal

Delighted
extinguished

Delivery
de outfits of de Palace staff

Demand
recently widowed

Demister
castration device

Dentist
someone who repairs car bodywork

Diabetes
to drop dead while making eyes at an insect

fig.26 Diabetes

Dd

Dialogue
an awful piece of wood

Diary
disappointing ecstasy tablet

Dictaphone
someone you don't like calling

Dictating
to leak milk from an unusual place

Diktat
shoddy condom

Dildo
pickle in pastry

fig.27 Disgruntled

Diphthong
fondue underwear

Dialogue–Ditto

Disarray
to give directions in China

Discover
Jamaican for duvet

Disgruntled
a pig with laryngitis

Disillusion
to slag off the work
of Paul Daniels

'you smell!'

Dismiss
to be rude to teacher

fig.28 Dismiss

Ditto
the Marx Brother who got fired because
he was too samey

Dd

Doctrine
your GP has arrived

Dog pound
a seventh of a human pound

Doldrum
an instrument to play while queuing at the DSS

Downsize
unit of feather measurement

Dubai
Debbie from Birmingham

Duck à l'orange
Get down! Ian Paisley's coming!

Dukedom
aristocratic birth control aid

fig.29 Downsize

1 down length

Doctrine–Dynamite

Dullard
a boring duck

Dumbstruck
a while van

Dumpling
small dump

Dunstable
to have shaved

Dynamite
to take a flea out for lunch

fig.30 Dullard

Ee

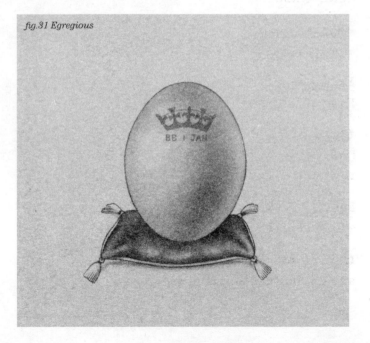

fig.31 Egregious

Ecstatic
moving now

Eeyore
a prostitute who advertises on the internet

Egregious
King of the eggs

Ejaculate
(Yorkshire) Greeting to husband on delayed
return from t'mill

Elate
a Spanish rowing crew

Elevenses
a Welsh bullfighting family

fig.32 Ecstatic

Ee

Email
(Yorkshire) 'The postman's arrived'

Emeralds
green piles

Emotions
virtual dumps

fig.33 Endorse

Enamour
what you use to bang nails in

Encyclopaedia
to be sexually attracted to small bikes

Endorse
loser in the Grand National

Engineer

a parking space next to your house

Enquire

a group of singing chickens from the East End

Entente cordiale

a happy French camper

Enunciate

to take Holy Orders loudly and clearly

Euthanasia

young people in China

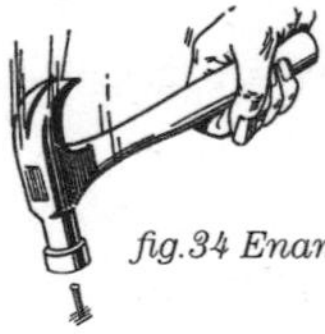

fig.34 Enamour

Excalibur

former drinker of non-alcoholic beer

Ee

Exceed
a plant

Expert
saggy

Extractor fan
former lover of agricultural equipment

Exceed

Seed

fig.35 Exceed

 **f**

fig.36 Flippertygibbet

Ff

Fallacy
1. amusingly shaped
2. cocky

Farting
Irish for 'a star'

Feckless
celibate in Ireland

fig.37 Felching

Felching
a successful insurance claim after falling down on the pavement

Fervent
a device required when tumble-drying cats

Fibre optic
a bartender's measure for muesli

Fallacy–Finesse

Fibula
a small lie

Figurine
butter substitute made from figs

Filibuster
clumsy vet

Fillip
a great boost for
the Queen

fig.38 Fervent

Filofax
pastry so thin you
can send it by telephone

Finesse
a lady from Finland

Ff

Fish
a bit like an F

Fishiest
someone who doesn't believe in cod

Fixate
to sabotage a rowing crew

Flabbergasted
appalled at your weight gain

Flagrant
a tramp with a whip

Flatterer
a rolling pin

Flemish
rather like snot

fig.39 Fishiest

Fish–Forswear

fig. 40 Flotilla

Flippertygibbet
dolphin gallows

Florida
more red in the face

Flotilla
an amphibious ape

Foodstuff
the meat is hard to cut

Forebear
look out there's a bear on the golf course!

Foreplay
wood popular in Knightsbridge

Forswear
army uniform

Ff

Founder member
result of rummaging in your Y fronts

Foxglove
Basil Brush

Francophile
Spanish dictator's medical records

Freebie
an unattached insect

Frowning
Herr Ning's wife

Frugal
a search engine for fruit

Fundamentalist
give money to David Icke

fig.41 Freebie

Founder member–Fungi

Fungal

good female company

Fungi

good male company

fig.42 Fungal and Fungi

Gg

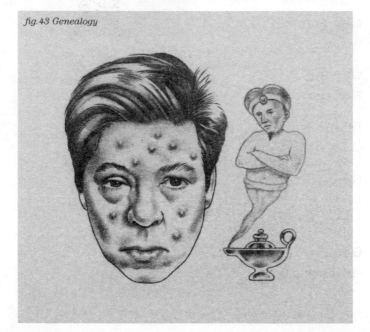

fig.43 Genealogy

Gastric
lighting a fart

Gastronome
flatulent elf

Gaucho
Mexican Marx Brother

fig. 44 Genteel

Gearstick
clothes glue

Genealogy
medical reaction to figures who appear
from magic lamps

Genteel
chivalrous fish

Gg

Gentile
ceramics around a urinal

Geriatric
the next time Germany starts a war

Germanic
mad virus

fig. 45 Goblet

Ghost
expression of astonishment
in an Indian restaurant

Ghoulish
Hungarian stew that comes back to haunt you

Giggle
very small music event

Goatherd
exclamation when flushing

Goblet
a small mouth

Gondolier
something you catch from a boatman

Goody bag
Jade's mother

fig.46 Gooseberry

Gooseberry
a big duck's hat

Grandee
recipient of £1000

Granule
Santa Claus' mother

Gg

Gravy
close to death

Gringo
Mexican drummer

Groin
the 'go' light in Birmingham

fig.47 Gravy

Gyroscope
a device for locating dole money

h

fig.48 Hat-trick

Hh

Hailstone
formal greeting for Sir Mick Jagger

Hairy
a bit like a German

Halitosis
smelly comet

Hamas
what Geordies use
to bang nails in

Hammer
Alan Rickman

Haphazard
mind the hap

fig. 49 Haphazard

Hailstone–Homosexual

Hat-trick
a pile of freshly mown hats

Heave ho
laughing till you're sick

Henna
like a hen but even more so

Himalaya
a transsexual rooster

Hoedown
agricultural strike

Homophone
gay chat line

Homosexual
randy Simpson's fan

fig.50 Himalaya

Hh

Honolulu
to give an MBE to a Scottish singer

Hootenanny
to boo Mary Poppins

Hopscotch
one-legged Glaswegian

Hornby
a sexy bee

Hosanna
a loose girl's name

Hypotenuse
the lavatory's engaged

Hysterical
fear of snakes

fig.51 Hopscotch

 **i**

fig.52 Iconoclastic

Ii

Icon
optical illusion

Iconoclastic
a rubber band for securing religious paintings

Imitate
pretend to be an art gallery

Impending
death of a pixie

Impolite
to set fire to a pixie

Import
what posh elves drink after dinner

Incarnation
immersed in condensed milk

fig.53 Imitate

Increment
bad Japanese weather

Indulgence
at a boring urinal

Industrialize
to write the words 'clean me' on the bonnet of
someone's car

Ineffable
something you can't swear about

Infantry
a baby oak

Inhabit
dressed as a monk

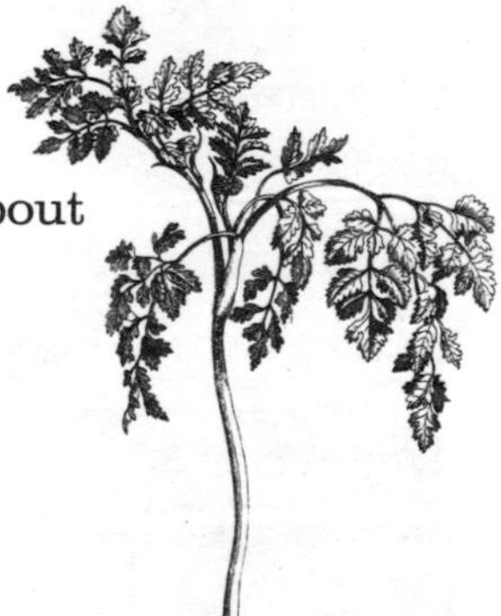

fig.54 Infantry

Ii

Institute
a freeze-dried hooker

Integrates
a fireplace enthusiast

Interfere
lover of horror movies

fig.55 Integrates

Intersperse
supports Tottenham

Intifada
a chain of West Bank florists

Investigate
pensions scandal

Inviolate
dressed in purple

Iris
short Dubliner

Ivy
Roman for four

fig.56 Ivy

Jj, Kk

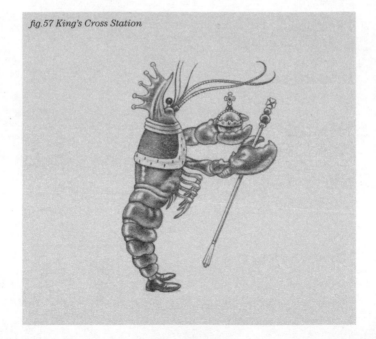

fig.57 King's Cross Station

Jacuzzi
Italian version of famous essay by Emile Zola

Jocular
Scots vampire

Jugular
a busty vampire

King's Cross Station
a Royal lobster

Kitsch
a small kitchen

Jj, Kk

Knacker's yard
enormous underpants

Knapsack
a sleeping bag

Kneepads
Scottish turnip commercials

Knick-knack
an ability to steal

fig.58 Knacker's Yard

 **l**

fig.59 Laburnum

Ll

La vie en rose
pink toilet

Labour
Tory

Laburnum
a French barbecue

fig. 60 Largesse

Laggard
a prison warder

Lamentable
(Yorkshire) 'The Sunday roast is ready'

Laplander
a clumsy private dancer

Largesse
a large 'S'

La vie en rose–Lockjaw

Lavish
a bit like a toilet

Leotard
an idiot in lycra

fig.61 Leotard

Liability
political skill

Listless
upright

Liveable
where Scousers come from

Lockjaw
the correct emergency procedure for disabling
Brian Blessed

Ll

Loiter
device used by smokers in the West Country

Looming
valuable antique Chinese lavatory

Louche
where Sean Connery goes when he's taken short

Lovelorn
to be very, very fond of grass

fig. 62 Looming

Mm

fig. 6.3 Mutant

Mm

Macho
device used by smokers in Spain

Maisonette
small lodge member

Majestic
a sceptre

Malady
a bit like a duck

Malcontent
someone who's perfectly happy with Malcolm

Malfunction
a party in a shopping centre

Malleable
matrimonially available Chinese lady

Malcolm

fig. 64 Malcontent

Macho–Maternity

Mange tout
seconds please

Manifesto
Jewish conjuror

Marinade
soft drink for weddings

Maritime
a wedding

Marmalade
the cry of a new-born chick

Mastication
sealant abuse

Maternity
(Yorkshire) 'It's my go at golf'

fig. 65 Maritime

Mm

fig.66 Misprint

Mattress–Mendacity

Mattress
a female mat

Maypole
Possibly Polish (see *Tadpole*)

Measles
what artists use for self-portraits

Megawatt
PARDON!?

Melancholy
fruit and veg

Memsahib
the same Swedish car

Mendacity
urban renewal programme

fig.67 Measles

Mm

Metatarsals
got together at Jeffrey Archer's

Miasma
the reason I have an inhaler

Microbe
a tiny dressing gown

Midwifery
part way through breaking wind

Minsk
camp Russian walk

Miscomprehension
winner of the English Grammar beauty contest

Misfit
a great-looking teacher

Midwif

fig.68 Midwifery

Metatarsals–Mitosis

Mishmash
to be late for chapel due to drunkenness

Misprint
to run in the wrong direction

Missile
an air stewardess

Mississippi
wife of Mister Ippi

Missive
South African for very big

fig. 69 Missile

Mistake
winner of the meat traders' beauty contest

Mitosis
what's on the end of my feetsis

Mm

Morass
putting on weight

Motorist
a painful condition affecting drivers

Mountaineer
a very specialized taxidermist

Mumps
heaps of unwanted mothers

Mutant
cross between a cat and an insect

MySpace
a hole in the skirting board

Mystery
a bit like a man

fig. 70 MySpace

Nn, Oo

fig. 71 Offset

Nn, Oo

Navigate
scandal concerning road diggers

Nicorette
skimpy briefs

Nobleman
eunuch

Noisette
a small noise

Notable
you'll have to have your dinner on the floor

fig. 72 Notable

Nubile
recent speech by Ian Paisley

Nutcase
a hat

Oboe
American tramp

Offset
the regulatory body that inspects badgers

Onomatopoeia
the first sign of a weak bladder

Onus
a very round bottom

Optical
to giggle during surgery

Optimist
the view through a cataract

Orienteering
court case in Japan

fig. 73 Nutcase

Nn, Oo

Oscillate
Rolf Harris hasn't turned up

Otter
nice weather in Yorkshire

fig. 74 Oscillate

Pp

fig 75 Parapet

Pp

Painful
complete with windows

Palaver
complicated knitting pattern

Palmistry
not knowing who your Dad is

fig. 76 Paradox

Paltry
a skinny chicken

Pancreas
a gland located next to King's Cross

Pantaloon
underwear fetishist

Paradox
flying doctors

Painful–Pastiche

Parapet
an airborne cat

Paraquat
a species of parrot that nobody likes

Parenthood
split condom

Participation
when your Dad joins in

fig.77 Paraquat

Particles
Ma's taken her feather duster to him again

Pasta
Italian priest

Pastiche
what Sean Connery eats in Cornwall

Pp

Peccadillo
an armour-plated condom

Pending
the noise of a brass biro

Pendulum
storage room for biros

Pentagram
occult stripper

Pentecost
that biro'll set you back

fig. 78 Pentagram

Pepper pot
a pot belonging to one who stutters

Perfect
the cat's pregnant

Peccadillo–Phlegmatic

Permutation
the theory of how hairdos evolved

Persist
a bag snatcher

Pharmacist
Old MacDonald had a boil

Philander
the Duke of Edinburgh and the Queen

Philanthropist
a kindly drunk

Philharmonic
to feed the Queen

Phlegmatic
battery-powered handkerchief

fig. 79 Perfect

Pp

fig.80 Peccadillo

Piccaninny–Pillory

Piccaninny
the FA selection process for choosing an England manager

Pie crust
what you get if you don't polish your pike

Piece-meal
dinner after a row

Pigsticking
clockwork pork

Pilgrim
depressive drug

Pillory
chemist

fig.81 Pigsticking

Pp

Pinnacle
the humane slaughter of kitchen aprons

Pinprick
not well endowed

Pistachio
the facial hair you might find on the top
lip of an alcoholic

Placebo
the Marx Brother who was fired because
people only *thought* he was good

Placenta
Japanese TV host

Platypus
to give your cat pigtails

fig.82 Platypus

Pinnacle–Precipice

PMT
afternoon refreshment

Polaroids
unpleasant ailment in arctic conditions

Poly-tunnel
parrot mine

Ponderous
shop that sells ponds

fig.83 PMT

Postmistress
sex by correspondence course

Potent
a camping convenience

Precipice
push-button toilet

91

Pp

Pretence
the days before camping

Prickly
a bit like George Galloway

Privilege
an outdoor loo on the tenth floor

Problematic
a disastrous loft conversion

Proboscis
against the workers

Prodigal
to poke a seabird

fig.84 Prodigal

Pretence–Prosaic

Profiteering
controversial item of jewellery in the shape
of Mohammed

Profundity
to like a silly little song

Prolapse
in favour of having your
dinner in front of the telly

Propaganda
a good look

fig.85 Propaganda

Property
the tea they say you can only get in Yorkshire

Prosaic
written by someone on antidepressants

Pp

Prosthetic
not a very good call girl

Protests
call-girl exams

Psychological
something that makes sense on a bike

Pubescent
intimate deodorant

Pulpit
what to do with a Jeffrey Archer novel

Punish
rather like a pun

Pyromaniac

one who collects glass baking dishes

fig.86 Psychological

Qq, Rr

fig.87 Rambling

Quest–Ratatouille

Quest
the Jonathan Ross family coat of arms

Rambling
jewellery for sheep

Ramsgate
Farming scandal

Rancour
Japanese term of abuse

Randomize
a squint

fig.88 Randomize

Ransom
a half-hearted jog

Ratatouille
the sound made by a machine-gun ricochet

Qq, Rr

Receptacle
playful welcome from the lady at the front desk

Reincarnation
born again as a tin of condensed milk

Reindeer
polite weather forecast

Replica
to suck up to the woman
from Thomas Cook

Repository
warehouse with
delivery at the back

Reproach
to harvest fish

fig.89 Reproach

Receptacle–Rotterdam

Republican
get a new barman

Resource
get some more ketchup

Rev counter
survey of vicars

Revelation
joy experienced when the car starts

Rind
what Prince Charles buys in a pub

fig.90 Rev counter

Robust
Japanese sagging breasts

Rotterdam
construction to prevent the flow of Terry-Thomas

Qq, Rr

Roulette
a queen

Routine
an adolescent kangaroo

Rubicon
imitation gemstone

Rumination
Australia

fig 91 Seesaw

Ss

Sago
a good way to start a race

Sanctity
multiple-breasted Frenchwoman

Sandy
that's convenient

Satire
when you're at the top table

fig.92 Sandy

Scandals
sandals with socks

Scapegoat
Muslim (soon to be Bulgarian)

Sago–Seesaw

Scar tissue

a problem attaching a DVD machine to the television

Scatological

an intelligent jazz riff

fig.93 Sea lion

Scrap

it is not very good

Scurrilous

a mouse with no legs

Sea lion

an implement for pressing seals

Seesaw

what Moses might have used to part the Red Sea

Ss

Semolina
a system of signalling with puddings

Senile
what to do in Egypt

Serial killer
combine harvester

fig.94 Semolina

Serviette
a bloke from Communist Russia

Sex
what the Queen keeps her coal in

Shagpile
an experience both painful and pleasant

Shambolic
false testicle

Senile–Shambolic

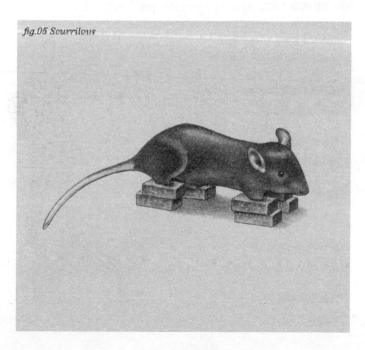

fig.05 Sourrilous

Ss

Shampoo
imitation bear

Shamrock
polystyrene boulder

Silicone
Madonna's bra

Ski lift
the elation you feel after eating a yoghurt

Skid
a baby goat on ice

Smirks
Geordie cigarettes

fig.96 Skid

Snuff box
coffin

Shampoo–Splinter

Soaring
the curry was too hot

Sometime
Maths lesson

Sorcerer
even more of a saucer

Soulmate
Korean bride

Specimen
Italian astronauts

fig.97 Sorcerer

Speculate
24-hour opticians

Splinter
Chinese 100-metre runner

Ss

Spoof
person who is only pretending to be homosexual

Sporran
what Scottish frogs do in ponds

Squeamish
a bit like a squeam

Statuette
what was it that you had for dinner?

Stifle
a lot of pigs

Stifling
Scottish dance for pigs

Stipend
pig house with a fence round it

fig.98 Spoof

Spoof–Surcharge

Stockade
fizzy Oxo

Stopgap
to campaign against competitively-priced denim

Stymie
a Jewish pig

Subdued
a less than cool person

Suffocate
East Anglian postcode

Suitable
a cow

fig 99 Suitable

Surcharge
what you pay for a knighthood

Ss

Sweepstake
what Sooty cooks for dinner

Syllabus
Liverpool coach

Symbolic
my mobile phone's on the blink

Syrupy
it might be a wig

Systematic
a robot nun

fig.100 Syrupy

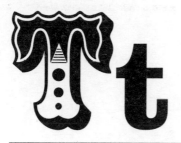

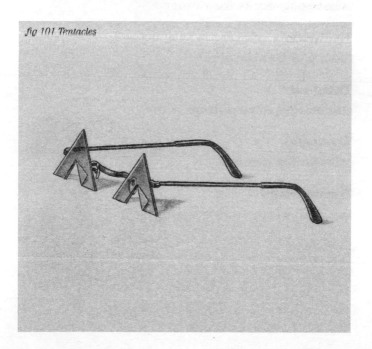

fig 101 Tentacles

Tt

Tadpole
ever so slightly Polish

Tailback
post-operative Manx cat

Tally-ho
a loose woman who keeps count

Tentacles
eyewear for campers

Terminology
the study of fur from Yorkshire

Terrapin
scary brooch

fig. 102 Tally-ho

Tadpole–Tissues

Tête-à-tête
to walk from one end of an art gallery to another

Thesaurus
condition caused by eating the hot curry

Tiddlywinks
a nap after a good drink

Tinker
an Irish philosopher

fig. 103 Tiddlywinks

Tirade
a puncture call-out service

Tissues
matters of importance in Yorkshire

Tt

Titillate
delayed puberty

Torpid
unfinished torpedo

Toucan
a couple of tins

Trail mix
to stalk Irishmen

Transcendental
cross-dressing dentist (see also 'tooth fairy')

Transgression
when female impersonators get cross

fig.104 Torpid

114

Titillate–Twinge

Transistor

a nun with surprisingly large hands

Trinidad

reply to the question:
'Which of those two
fashion experts do you
fancy, son?'

Tumbling

a belly-button ring

Turbine

windy headgear

fig. 105 Transistor

Twinge

what Sean Connery calls siblings of the same age

Tt

Twofold
beginners' origami class

Typhoon
tea that gives you wind

Tyrant
angry reaction to being told you have to wear a tie

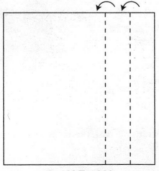

fig.106 Twofold

Uu, Vv

fig 107 Venezuela

Uu, Vv

Uganda
go and have a look

Uncoil
a French contraceptive

fig. 108 Uniform

Undeterred
a skidmark

Ungrateful
a blazing fire in France

Uniform
having the shape of a female sheep

Unscrew
French prison warder

Uganda–Vigilant

Urchin

where Anne Robinson keeps her beard

Urethra

a soul singer who takes the piss

Varicose

nearby

Venezuela

a gondola with a harpoon

Vigilant

an insect that stays
up all night

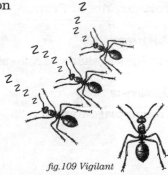

fig.109 Vigilant

Uu–Vv

Violin
nasty pub

Virgin Broadband
a chaste female musical group

Virgin olive oil
Popeye's fiancée

fig. 110 Violin

W w

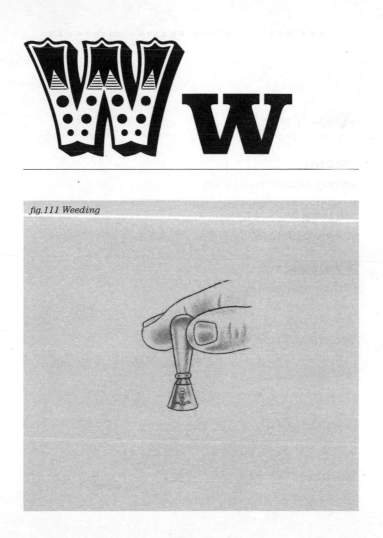

fig.111 Weeding

Ww

Walnut
an obsessive bricklayer

Walrus
last exclamation of Russell's driving instructor

Warbling
Geordie jewellery

Warming
Geordie porcelain

Warthogs
Geordie clothing

fig.112 Wastrel

Washington
a substantial amount of laundry

Wastrel
a very idle bird of prey

Walnut–Winsome

WC2
downstairs cloakroom

Weeding
Scottish handbell

Wholefood
a doughnut

Wicked
evil cricket equipment

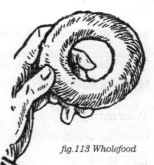

fig.113 Wholefood

Windbreak
backward fart

Winnebago
a horse with a bad back

Winsome
partial success

Ww

Wisteria
a nostalgic form of panic

Witchcraft
1. Anne Robinson's boat;
2. magazine for boat owners

Wormcast
a downloadable
worm

Worsted
unpopular bear

fig.114 Worsted

Xx, Yy, Zz

fig.115 Zucchini

Xx, Yy, Zz

X-rated
no longer appreciated

Yacht
a negative yes

Yeoman
presidential greeting

Yo!
a yoyo that only goes one way

Yodelling
trainee Jedi knight

Zucchini
animal-park enthusiast

fig. 116 Yo!